shiarightswatch   shiarightswatch   shiarightswatch   shiarightswatch

Shia Rights Watch envisions the world with peace for all humans, regardless of their religion, gender, race and origin. There should be regulations in every country to support every religion. We believe Shia Muslim as religion should be recognized in every country and any discrimination should be brought to light. God has given us all the freedom of religion and the rights to live in peace.

Shia Rights Watch

1050 17th St NW Suite 800

Washington, DC 20036

Tel: +1 (202) 350 4302 Or 202-643 SHIA

srwdc@ShiaRightsWatch.org

Established in 2011, Shia Rights Watch (SRW) is the world's first independent organization dedicated to define and protect the rights of Shia Muslims around the world. SRW is a non- governmental, not-for-profit research entity and advocacy group headquartered in Washington D.C., U.S.A. Shia Rights Watch holds a 501(c) status, as well as holding a Special consultation status (ECOSOC) with the United Nations. Shia Rights Watch aims to draw the international attention where Shia rights are violated; the aim is to give a voice to the oppressed and hold oppressors accountable for their crimes. S.R.W. achieves its objectives through strategic investigations supported by targeted advocacy in order to bring about informed action.

Vision

Freedom of religion for all

Shia Rights Watch envisions the world with peace for all humans, regardless of their religion, gender, race and origin. There should be regulations in every country to support every religion. We believe Shia Muslim as religion should be recognized in every country and any discrimination should be brought to light. God has given us all the freedom of religion and the rights to live in peace.

Mission

No Shia above the law and no Shia Below the law

Shia Rights Watch is dedicated to protect the rights of Shia Muslims worldwide. We investigate violations against Shia communities in order to raise awareness against injustice. We promote change through research and publications. Our reports and articles are submitted to governments and international organizations, and we continually monitor media outlets to ensure coverage of Shia rights violations. Shia Rights Watch stands for victims of prejudice, and supports activism in order to prevent discrimination, support political freedom, and protect people from inhumane conduct. We enlist the local public and international communities to support the cause of human rights for all.

The Purpose of SRW

Shia Muslims face constant oppression throughout the world solely based on their faith. In some countries, Shia Muslims have been the target of repeated persecution for centuries as evidenced in the well-documented expansion of extremism of the Wahhabi movement. We believe the underrepresented Shia Muslim population need a human rights organization that highlights the violations against them, while giving their call for help a louder voice.

Staff Organization

The organization began with the collaborative efforts of volunteers with a common interest in advocating international human rights. The momentum created by the increasing number of volunteer and activism allowed for a formal development of the foundation of Shia Rights Watch. Currently the organization has more than 600 active members working in various locations worldwide. The responsibilities of members range from gathering news and information to publishing reports and articles in order to advocate change. We are proud of the religiously and ethnically diverse group of activists who are working together towards a common goal.

Methodology of SRW

We believe that information is the most valuable resource in the investigative process. From the organization's inception, we have focused on gathering information through various media: interviewing witnesses, family members of the victims and victims themselves; on-site collection of resources; analyzing reports from various national and international organizations; meeting with non-governmental and religious organizations, leaders, and journalists; and creating information networks in a wide range of social sectors.

Based on the information collected from the above sources, different types of human rights violation have been identified. These violations include, but are certainly not limited to:

Violation of right of living;

Arbitrary arrest, unfair trial, and illegal detention;

Psychical & psychological abuse: torture, rape, and sexual assault;

Illegal confiscation of private property;

Demolition of Religions centers;

Employment discrimination;

Education discrimination;

Reports, Publications, and Distribution

Whether it is terrorist bombings of sacred shrines, torture and unjust detention of people, discriminative legislation or intimation of school children for their religious beliefs, Shia have been victimized in most the world. In countries where the press is tightly controlled, most of these cases go unnoticed. Shia Rights Watch tells the stories of injustices and atrocities in order to give a voice to the marginalized Shia victims.

Journalists investigating topics regarding the Middle East will benefit from SRW's focus on the Shia communities since they are crucially important sectors in Middle Eastern society. For instance, In order to fully examine the ongoing atrocities committed against protesters of the Arab spring, it is necessary to know about the embedded Shia struggle. In areas where Shia have been formerly discriminated against more subtly, the Arab Spring opened a door for more blunt persecution. Cases reported in other parts of the world, such as in South Asia, describe violence and intimidation which reflect fluctuating trends in hostilities, fueled by various political issues, including terrorism. SRW's aim is to be able to report the crimes affecting Shia in every part of the globe.

SRW has investigators on the forefront who communicate directly with the victims and monitor multilingual news media outlets. SRW networks with national committees, international human rights organizations, as well as religious scholars of Shia communities. SRW's members comprise of people with diverse ethnic and religious backgrounds united to defend the human rights. This international network provides invaluable information to commentators and journalists of the media who are seeking to explore the impact of events on the Shia communities worldwide.

Bahrain: The Forgotten Revolution
The Persecution of Shia Muslims

Contents

Creeds and Origins

In Bahrain, approximately 70% of the population are Muslim, with the 30% remaining being that of Hindu, Buddhism, Jews, and Christians, alike. The majority of Muslims are Shia, with Sunni making up less than 5% of the entire Muslim population.[1] In Bahrain, the Shia population are commonly divided into two main ethnic groups: Bahraini and Ajam. Those who fall under the Bahraini Shia population, are historically native to Bahrain; whereas, most Ajam's have emigrated from Iran to Bahrain over the century. The Al-Khalifa royal family are predominantly Sunni Muslims, even though Bahrain is one of five countries to pertain to a Shia majority, with most belonging to Twelver Sects of Ithna'Ashari. Thus, due to the Sunni minority maintaining rule, Shia's are consistently persecuted and killed on a basis of faith.

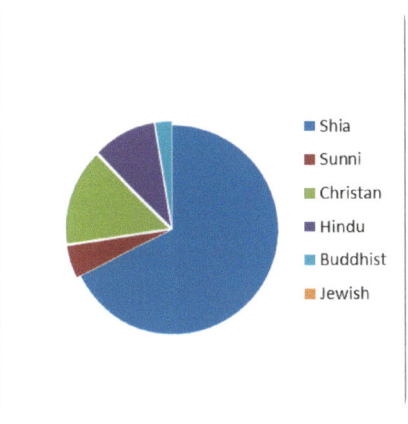

Political Uprisings of 2011 (Bahrain's Reaction to the Arab Spring)

What started as a peaceful protest petitioning equal rights among Bahraini citizens turned into a mass bloodshed with the Bahraini government willfully murdering their citizens. After seeing the many successful protests that took place during the Arab Spring in places such as Egypt and Tunisia, many Bahrain citizens gained hope in deciding to stand up and make a name for themselves in protest of the corrupt Al-Khalifa regime. Bahraini's protested in regards to forming a democratic state where Shia would no longer be persecuted for their faith. Most of the protests demonstrating their contest of the Khalifa regime remained peaceful, carrying flowers as a sign of this accord. However, government forces rejected this unity and instead took to violence, defying a profusion of articles of the Universal Declaration of Human Rights in which Bahrain had signed onto in 1998.

During the Bahraini uprisings, Bahrain security forces, along with those of Saudi Arabia brought in to repress the violence, breached the human rights of thousands of Bahraini citizens by inflicting excessive force on amicable protestors, including that of women and children. Since the insurrections, the Bahraini government has been convicted of consistently executing a variety of human rights eludes. These contraventions include: lack of due process, torture, sexual assault, the detaining of children, lethal force, as well as a myriad of other violations that pertain to the articles of the UDHR.[2]

The Bahrain Independent Commission of Inquiry (BICI)

The Bahrain Independent Commission of Inquiry (BICI), also known locally in Bahrain as the Bassiouni Commission, was established by Hamad Bin Isa Al-Khalifa, prevailing King of Bahrain, on the 29th of June, 2011. The BICI was

[1] N.A. *World Atlas.* N.D. http://www.worldatlas.com/webimage/countrys/asia/bh.htm

[2] "Bahrain." Human Rights Watch. N.D. http://www.hrw.org/world-report/2014/country-chapters/bahrain

tasked with looking into the incidents that occurred during the period of unrest in Bahrain from February and March of 2011, as well as the consequences of these events. The commission released a 500-page report on November 23rd, 2011, which took 9,000 testimonies, offered an extensive chronology of events, documented 46 deaths, 559 allegations of torture, and more than 4,000 cases of employees dismissed for participating in the protests of 2011. The BICI offered numerous recommendations to King Hamad regarding the accordance of past violations, as well as endorsements on preventing future ones. Although the King immediately welcomed the various accusations and recommendations brought on by BICI, many human rights organizations have since found that less than five of these recommendations have been implemented. This lack of implementation has led the king to have since been widely criticized for the mass amounts of violence to continuously take place within the Bahraini kingdom.[3]

Treaties and Documents

In 1998, Bahrain signed on to the Universal Declaration of Human Rights (UDHR) which consists of 30 articles intendant on protecting the rights of individuals worldwide. Bahrain has also ratified the Convention on the Rights of a Child in 1992[4] and the International Covenant on Civil and Political Rights in 2006.[5] Bahrain has further established a constitution that advocates direct protection for the rights of all Bahraini citizens. However, in recent years, specifically proceeding the uprisings of the Arab Spring in 2011, Bahrain has failed to enforce these documents, inflicting vast human rights abuses upon its citizens. Not only is Bahrain encroaching documents they have personally adopted, such as the UDHR and Convention on the Rights of a Child and the International Covenant on Civil and Political Rights, but they are in direct violation of their constitution.

[3] "Bahrain Independent Commission of Inquiry." *BICI,* N.D. http://www.bici.org.bh/

[4] "Chapter IV Human Rights." *UN.* 2014. https://treaties.un.org/Pages/ViewDetails.aspx?mtdsg_no=IV-11&chapter=4&lang=en

[5] "Chapter IV Human Rights." *UN.* 2014. https://treaties.un.org/pages/viewdetails.aspx?chapter=4&src=treaty&mtdsg_no=iv-4&lang=en

Summary

The following pages are direct examples of specific rights of Bahraini citizens that are being abused forthright by the Bahraini authorities. Furthermore, disclaiming that although this document cites numerous direct examples of conflict wreaked upon Bahraini citizens, there are plentiful instances of citizens being harmed that are not documented within these pages. This lack of evidence is welcomed by the notion that Bahrain continues to be the dominant country in advocating for protection of its officials by funding and obtaining the largest amount of attorneys, as well as intelligently securing their actions through profound legal actions. An exemplary form of this malicious behavior is cited in the case of Abdulhadi al-Khawaja who is currently serving a life sentence, along with 13 other high profile human rights activists, on a basis of alleged allocations of "terrorism." Shia Rights Watch, through extensive research, has constructed that accusations of terrorism often result to peaceful actions of protesting for democracy that are legally defined as "plots to overthrow the regime." Put simply, citizens are arrested because they do not agree with the Bahraini government's mass impairment towards its citizens and thus want them out of power; which under Bahraini law, is delineated as "terrorism," with further, unambiguous cases shown in the following pages.

Documented Cases of Violations

Arbitrary Arrest

In 1998, Bahrain signed onto the Universal Declaration of Human Rights (UDHR) which states:

Article 9.

No one shall be subjected to arbitrary arrest, detention or exile.

Article 11.

(1) Everyone charged with a penal offence has the right to be presumed innocent until proved guilty according to law in a public trial at which he has had all the guarantees necessary for his defence.

(2) No one shall be held guilty of any penal offence on account of any act or omission which did not constitute a penal offence, under national or international law, at the time when it was committed. Nor shall a heavier penalty be imposed than the one that was applicable at the time the penal offence was committed.[6]

Bahrain also ratified the International Covenant on Civil and Political Rights (ICCPR) in 2006, declaring the following international law:

Article 9.

1. Everyone has the right to liberty and security of person. No one shall be subjected to arbitrary arrest or detention. No one shall be deprived of his liberty except on such grounds and in accordance with such procedure as are established by law.

2. Anyone who is arrested shall be informed, at the time of arrest, of the reasons for his arrest and shall be promptly informed of any charges against him.

3. Anyone arrested or detained on a criminal charge shall be brought promptly before a judge or other officer authorized by law to exercise judicial power and shall be entitled to trial within a reasonable time or to release. It shall not be the general rule that persons awaiting trial shall be detained in custody, but release may be subject to guarantees to appear for trial, at any other stage of the judicial proceedings, and, should occasion arise, for execution of the judgement.

4. Anyone who is deprived of his liberty by arrest or detention shall be entitled to take proceedings before a court, in order that that court may decide without delay on the lawfulness of his detention and order his release if the detention is not lawful.

---

[6] "The Universal Declaration of Human Rights." *United Nations,* N.D. http://www.un.org/en/documents/udhr/

5. Anyone who has been the victim of unlawful arrest or detention shall have an enforceable right to compensation.[7]

However, although Bahrain has adopted the previous principles as international law, does not mean they have practiced them. In fact, various cases documented since 2011 proves that Bahrain has yet to reform. The following are cases document within 2014 of Bahraini citizens who were arbitrarily arrested.

Cases of Arbitrary Arrests:

1) **April 14th:** Police detained 19 people without warrant during a raid in a Bahraini village; 17 of the arrested were detained during a home raid, while the other 7 were arrested on the street, including 6 children, ages ranging between 12 and 14, who were arrested at a check point in the Daih area. The children include:

> *Muhammad Shakir 12 years old*
>
> *Hussain Mashi'a 12 years old*
>
> *Ahmed Hani 12 years old*
>
> *Ali Shamloh 13 years old*
>
> *Ja'afar Hani 14 years old*
>
> *Wadi'a Wadiee (age unknown)*

2) **June 8th:** Bahrain's main opposition group, Al-Wefaq's new report contends that more than 7,300 people have been arrested since this time last year, including that of 214 children during raids on their homes and schools.

3) **August 18th:** More than 22 activists are imprisoned for their role in protests against the Al-Khalifa regime.

4) **September 1st:** Top Shiite Human Rights Activist, is Maryam al-Khawaja arrested for allegedly assaulting a police officer immediately upon entrance into the country with prospects of visiting her jailed human rights activist father, Abdulhadi al-Khawaja, who is currently serving a life sentence as a result of an unfair trial. Maryam further claims that she was assaulted upon arrest, resulting in a torn muscle in her shoulder. [8]

5) **September 16th:** Bahraini citizen, Tawfeeq Al Towk has disappeared; relatives are unable to find his whereabouts or contact him. [9]

6) **September 22nd:** 27 people were arrested between September 22nd-28th, including 9 women and 2 children.[10]

---

[7] "Chapter IV Human Rights." *UN.* 2014. https://treaties.un.org/pages/viewdetails.aspx?chapter=4&src=treaty&mtdsg_no=iv-4&lang=en

[8] "Maryam Al-Khawaja's Arrest Shows Bahrain at its worst." *The Guardian,* 2nd September, 2014. http://www.theguardian.com/commentisfree/2014/sep/02/maryam-alkhawaja-arrest-bahrain-us-uk

[9] "Bahrain Detainees Make Telephone Calls to their Relatives at the Criminal Investigations Headquarters, and then Disappear for Days." *Bahrain Rights,* 16th September, 2014. http://www.bahrainrights.org/en/node/7063

[10] "Bahrain Weekly Newsletter 71." *ADHRB,* 29th September, 2014. http://adhrb.org/2014/09/bahrain-weekly-newsletter-71/

7) **October 1ˢᵗ:** Prominent Human Rights Activist, Nabeel Rajab is arrested and scheduled to face trial on accusations of insulting the regime via a twitter post.[11]

8) **October 10ᵗʰ:** Bahraini authorities express systemic repression in the arrest and detainment of recently detained Bahraini citizen's 26 year old brother. Mahmood Suroor is arrested on October 10ᵗʰ, 2014. Mahmood had disappeared for 5 days after masked Bahraini authorities raided his home and confiscated many of his belongings, including his cellphone, camera, and external hard drive. Mahmood was later transferred to Dry Docks Detention prison where he was sentenced to be held for 60 days pending investigation. [12]

9) **November 11ᵗʰ:** A second year medical student, Ahmed Fahad al-Tashani is arrested in the Bahraini airport while trying to board his flight back home to his university in Egypt. Sources confirm that in attempt to distract a false testimony, Al-Tashani was subject to brutal torture by the Criminal Investigation Directorate (CID). Al-Tashani was arrested with 16 other individuals, mostly children in middle or high school, of whom he did not know. Al-Tashani's mother further contends that her son has no involvement in political issues as he is academically motivated. Al-Tashani was released two days later pending adherence to travel bans. The charges against Al-Tashani remain.[13]

10) **November 22ⁿᵈ:** American born citizen of Connecticut, Tagi al-Maiden was arrested, tortured and detained upon a false statement allegedly collected while under torture inflicted pressure by Bahraini authorities. Al-Maiden was sentenced to a 10 year term and has received further ill treatment since his sentencing. Bahraini police state that al-Maiden was involved in an illegal protest in which they claim that he threw a stone at a police with the intent of killing him, participated in the destruction of police vehicles and was in possession of Molotov cocktails. Al-Maiden claims he was not at the scene of this protest and his parents have further credibly testified that he was in fact not there. However, under torture in the form of beating his chest, head, and having to endure standing for long periods, al-Maiden confessed to a false testimony stating that he did in fact take part in these events, thus resulting in a 10 year sentence.[14]

11) **December 9ᵗʰ:** On his way to visit the Islamic holy sites of Iraq and Saudi Arabia, award winning photographer, Sayed Baqer al-Kamel was arrested representing yet another attempt at systemic repression by the Bahraini government.[15]

12) **December 10ᵗʰ:** Shaikh Jaffar Abduljalil al-Meqdad, one of the 13 famously detained activists, Shaikh Abduljalil al-Meqdad, was arrested upon arrival to police station to report his passport as lost. As yet another attempt at systemic repression upon human rights activists and their families, security forces have charged Jaffar with assaulting a police officer. He was able to phone his family from the CID. [16]

---

[11] "Bahrain: Arrest of Leading Human Rights Defender Nabeel Rajab for Tweets." *ADHRB*, 1ˢᵗ October, 2014. http://www.bahrainrights.org/en/node/7096

[12] "Brothers Hussam and Suroor Targeted for Freedom of Expression in Bahrain." *ADHRB*, 28ᵗʰ October 2014.

[13] "Bahraini Student Arrested as He Left to Study in Egypt... and Charged Political Issue." *Alwasat*, 11ᵗʰ November 2014.

[14] "U.S. Concerned Over Alleged Torture of American in Bahraini Jail." *Edition*. 22ⁿᵈ November, 2014. http://edition.cnn.com/2014/11/21/justice/american-prisoner-bahrain/

[15] "Photographer Syed Baqir Full Arrest of Saudi Arabia Bridge." *Alwasat*. 11ᵗʰ December, 2014. http://www.alwasatnews.com/4478/news/read/943739/1.html

[16] "The Arrest of Sheikh Abdul Jalil al-Miqdad Son on Charges of Assault on a Security Patrol." *Alwasat*. 11ᵗʰ December, 2014. http://www.alwasatnews.com/4478/news/read/943713/1.html

13) December 14th: Seventeen Bahraini citizens were arrested, including three children on their way to visit Iraq. Sources did not give a reason for this arbitrary detention.[17]

14) December 28th: Leader of political opposition group, Sheikh Ali Salman was arrested following over 10 hours of interrogation just days after being reelected as leader of Al-Wefaq, the national Islamic society that is known in Bahrain as the Shia political group that strives to promote change through equality. Unsurprisingly, Salman has been accused of terrorist related charges amounting to trying to overthrow the regime through inciting hatred. [18]

Systemic Repression

Bahrain publically expressed its recognition of all people being equal before the law without discrimination in signing onto the Universal Declaration of Human Rights (UDHR) in 1998, adopting the following principles as practice they would enforce:

Article 1.

All human beings are born free and equal in dignity and rights. They are endowed with reason and conscience and should act towards one another in a spirit of brotherhood.[19]

Bahrain further recognized this notion in the ratification of the International Covenant on Civil and Political Rights in 2006. By ratification of this treaty, Bahrain acknowledged that they enforced the following articles into international law:

Article 26.

All persons are equal before the law and are entitled, without any discrimination, to the equal protection of the law. In this respect, the law shall prohibit any discrimination and guarantee to all persons equal and effective protection against discrimination on any ground such as race, color, sex, language, religion, political or other opinion, national or social origin, property, birth or other status.[20]

However, since the mass uprisings of 2011, Bahrain has continuously expressed systemic repression against its citizens in prospects of maintaining power within the corrupt Al-Khalifa regime. The following documented cases are occurrences that took place within 2014 of the Bahrain regime suppressing its citizens.

---

[17] Security Authorities to Release All Prisoners of the King Fahd Causeway and Keep the Two." *Alwasat,* 13th December, 2014. http://www.alwasatnews.com/4480/news/read/944243/1.html

[18] "Newly Re-elected Head of Al Wefaq Society Arrested." *Shia Post,* 28th December, 2014. http://en.shiapost.com/2014/12/28/newly-re-elected-head-of-al-wefaq-society-arrested/

[19] "The Universal Declaration of Human Rights." *United Nations,* N.D. http://www.un.org/en/documents/udhr/

[20] "Chapter IV Human Rights." *UN.* 2014. https://treaties.un.org/pages/viewdetails.aspx?chapter=4&src=treaty&mtdsg_no=iv-4&lang=en

February 11th: In Sitra, an island south of the capital of Manama, 12 Bahraini citizens were injured as police raided the village with shotgun pellets. Mohammed Sanadi was shot in the face as he opened the window of his home and pellets came raging at him.[21]

May 6th: Police forces terrorize wife and children of recent victim of the Bahrain regimes systemic repression, Issa Abdulhasan, who was killed by Bahraini authorities in 2011. Sources confirm that police forces arbitrarily broke into the Abdulhasan's home in the early morning hours in the Karzakan village. The family confirmed that the forces failed to present legal permission to enter and search the home. They also stated that there was no reason for the raid. Furthermore, authorities then raided the neighboring apartment belonging to the Abdulhasan's brother-in-law. Security forces allegedly broke in without prior warning while his wife was not wearing her head scarf. She was further questioned and insulted by the forces before they left, leaving the home in a mess.[22]

May 21st: Clash between Bahraini mourners and security forces broke out during a ceremony to mark the death of a Shia killed in a recent attack on May 16th, Ali Faisal al-Akrawi.

May 26th: 15 Bahraini citizens are killed during clash with police during a protest proceeding a funeral procession of a recently murdered Shiite activist. 14 year old Mahmoud Mohsen was struck in the heart and chest by buckshot pellets. Mohsen had been filming the protests on behalf of opposition activists.

May 28th: Government troops fired tear gas and birdshot pellets at protestors who gathered to commemorate the death of 14 year old Seyed Mahmood Seyed Mohsen who was killed by Bahraini authorities.[23]

June 2nd: Bahraini authorities release death certificate of Abdulazziz Alabbar who was recently killed by Bahraini authorities, with an erroneous cause of death. Al-Wefaq, the Bahraini regime's lead opposition group, publically demand the release of a death certificate mentioning the real cause of death. The individual responsible for killing Alabbar has not been charged with any crime.[24]

August 21st: U.S. Top Diplomat denied access into Bahrain in order to investigate ongoing human rights abuses.[25]

September 3rd: Photo journalist arrested for covering protest, instead charged with partaking in protest, to which him and his lawyer deny.

October 15th: Americans for Democracy and Human Rights in Bahrain (ADHRB) documents that during the first week of October the following took place: 14 arrests, 13 postponed trials, 20 protests and sit-ins, continued use of excessive force by regime.[26]

---

[21] "Bahraini Children not excluded from Official Violence." *Shia Post*, 11th February, 2014. http://en.shiapost.com/2014/02/11/bahraini-children-not-excluded-from-official-violence/

[22] "Bahrain Regime Forces Terrorize Families of Martyrs." *Tasnim News*, 6th May, 2014. http://www.tasnimnews.com/English/Home/Single/360994

[23] "Bahrain Forces Attack Anti-Regime Demonstrators." *ABNA*, 28th May, 2014. http://www.abna.ir/english/service/bahrain/archive/2014/05/28/611855/story.html

[24] "Bahrain: Corpse of Young Man 'Alabbar' Remain in Detention for 45th Day." *ABNA*, 2nd June, 2014. http://www.abna.ir/english/service/bahrain/archive/2014/06/02/612961/story.html

[25] "Testimony of Tom Malinowski before the Tom Lantos Human Rights Comission on the Implementation of the Bahrain Independent Commission of Inquiry Report." *HRW*, 1st August, 2014. http://www.hrw.org/news/2012/08/01/testimony-tom-malinowski-tom-lantos-human-rights-comission-implementation-bahrain-in

[26] "Weekly Report- 6 to 12 October." *ADHRB*, n.d. https://gallery.mailchimp.com/e6f34c0956814788aedb2040c/files/Weekly_Report_6_to_12_October_01.pdf

October 27th: In a recent report, The Bahraini Committee of Detained Athletes (BCDA) contends that at least 75 athletes have systemically been targeted and detained by Bahraini authorities. The BCDA suggests that Bahrain has since found that the systemic detainment of athletes who represent their country in events such as the national Olympics could potentially hurt their country rather than help. Thus, Bahraini authorities have since limited systemic repression of athletes. However, the 75 detained since 2011 have not been released, with one of these athletes, Hamad al-Fahd, being given a life sentence. The BCDA further suggests that the actual number of detained athletes, including those subject to life sentences, is in reality much higher; however, given the data they were from Bahrain, 74 is all they could verify. The list is as follows.

Bahraini Athletes Being Arbitrarily Detained:

1) Hamad al-Fahd
2) Jafar Collar
3) Hussein Abdul Ghani Alkabbat
4) Mohammed Mirza
5) Hassan Abdul Wahab Al-Khayat
6) Abdel Azim Abdullah Collar
7) Ahmed Abdullah collar
8) Ahmed Khozaz
9) Sadiq Jafar Jassim
10) Khalil Ali Sindi
11) Hussein Sari
12) Hassan Ghandi Hilarious
13) Aamer Anwar Juma
14) Ali Abd al-Hadi
15) Jalal Ahmed ali Minister
16) Sadiq Jafar Taki
17) Qasim Habib Abdullah
18) Adel Hassan
19) Younis Hussein
20) Ahmed Mohammed Habib
21) Ahmed Abdul
22) Hasan Abdullah
23) Baqer Mohammed Jawad Shihabi
24) Ibrahim Juma Ibrahim
25) Jaafar Mohammed Habib
26) Ahmded Ali Al-Attiyah
27) Faisal Ali Al-Attiyah
28) Hassan Ali Al-Attiyah
29) Mohsen Ibrahim al-Marzouq
30) Jalal Abbas Alanfoz
31) Ali Abbas Alanfoz
32) Amjad Ahmed Aloaill
33) Ahmed Hussein Shihabi
34) Ahmed Abdullah
35) Amer Salman Shihabi
36) Ali Mohammed Jayad
37) Ali Abbas Abdullah
38) Abdul Qadir al-Fatlawi
39) Mohannad Ali
40) Muhsin Mahdi
41) Ibrahim Ismail Shahabi
42) Adnan Majid Amiri
43) Syed ali Musa
44) Hassan Saleh Ali
45) Jassim Ramadan
46) Imran Majid Amiri
47) Hadi Mohammed Moradi
48) Hussein Mahdi
49) Hakeem Oraibi
50) Mohammed Khamis
51) Ahmed Hassan Abdul Wahab
52) Ahmed Hussain
53) Zia Salman Zayer
54) Ali Saeed
55) Reza Hassan Jassim
56) Younes Abdulkarim
57) Mehdi Ahmed Hassan
58) Hassan ali Jawad
59) Jassam Ahmed Hassan
60) Ibrahim Ahmed Hassan
61) Mahdi Muhsin ali Mahdi
62) Habib Issa Hassan Matter
63) Ibrahim Ali Ibrahim
64) Habib Abdullah Matar
65) Abdullah Abdalomiramona
66) Hussein Ahmed Damama
67) Yusuf Karim Indian
68) Abdullah Latif Singer
69) Hassan ali Ibrahim
70) Habib Ayoub aker
71) Hussein Ali Mehdi
72) Ali Akbar Alkachi
73) Syed Ali Syed Hashim
74) Fawzi Hassan Ali

November 22nd: A video posted online shows Bahraini police officers pull over car and beat a man, containing him to his car. Once the man is allowed to open the door, his shirt is stained with blood as he uses it to wipe the excess that is dripping down his face. Two more officers pull up. The man is handcuffed and driven off in police vehicles. [27]

November 27th: Bahrain Centre for Human Rights (BCHR) women's rights defender, Ghada Jansheer was rearrested just hours after her release from a 10 week incarceration. On November 27th, Jansheer was arrested on charges of "assaulting a police officer" back in September, while she was in prison. However, Jansheer claims to have no recollection of this instance and further states that she was never informed of these charges against her, as well as an investigation was never conducted. Several human rights organizations find this arrest to be arbitrary and systemic in linking to the upcoming International Day for the Elimination of Violence against Women on 11/29.[28]

The Inhumane Treatment of Children

In 1992, Bahrain ratified the Convention on the Rights of the Child, a document containing 41 articles that recognize the inherent right of all children born to the human race. [29] By ratifying this document, Bahrain publically announced its enforcement into international and Bahraini law. Bahrain has furthered signed onto the Universal Declaration of Human Rights (UDHR) in 1998, recognizing the inherent rights of all individuals as pertaining to the following articles:

Article 16.

(3) The family is the natural and fundamental group unit of society and is entitled to protection by society and the State.

Article 25.

(2) Motherhood and childhood are entitled to special care and assistance. All children, whether born in or out of wedlock, shall enjoy the same social protection.[30]

After signing onto the previous two documents, Bahrain further ratified the International Convention on Civil and Political Rights (ICCP), recognizing the following notions as part of Bahraini law:

---

[27] N.A. *Youtube.* 22nd November, 2014. https://www.youtube.com/watch?v=bbWM6unjRA8&feature=youtu.be

[28] "Women's Rights Defender Ghada Jansheer Released and Immediately Re-Arrested." *Shia Post.* 30th November, 2014. http://en.shiapost.com/2014/11/30/womens-rights-defender-ghada-jamsheer-released-and-immediately-re-arrested/

[29] See CRC.

[30] Also see: "Convention on Rights of the Child." Pg. 53

Article 24.

1. Every child shall have, without any discrimination as to race, colour, sex, language, religion, national or social origin, property or birth, the right to such measures of protection as are required by his status as a minor, on the part of his family, society and the State.

2. Every child shall be registered immediately after birth and shall have a name.

3. Every child has the right to acquire a nationality.[31]

However, since the uprisings of 2011, not only has Bahrain inflicted mass harm upon its citizens as a basis of persecution towards individuals protesting the corrupt regime, particularly that of Shia Muslims, Bahrain has gone to the further extent of incarcerating, torturing and even killing children, against the protection instated in the various documents they have signed onto. The following are cases of harm inflicted upon Bahraini children within the year of 2014.

Cases of Children Being Denied Their Inherent Right of Protection:

March 22nd: Bahraini authorities arrest 12 year old Qassim Mohammed and Mohammed Ahmed. Both boys are being charged for their involvement in a peaceful gathering.[32]

March 31st: 13 Bahraini teenagers, ages 16-18, were given life-imprisonment on charges of attempting to murder a police officer by attacking their vehicle, as well as partaking in an illegal protest. Sources verify that the majority of the accused claimed innocence in the charges of participating in the attacks. [33]

May 20th: Bahraini authorities detain two children, ages 11 and 13 on charges of illegal gathering. Bahraini police arrested the brothers, Mohamed Hussain (11) and Ali Hussain (13) in their neighborhood of Nuwidrat.

May 20th: Eleven year old, Jehad Nabeel Al-Sameea was arrested from his neighborhood of Sanabis by Bahraini forces during their raid on a peaceful protest. Al-Sameea was charged with rioting, illegal gathering, possession of Molotov cocktails, damaging police cars and physically assaulting a police officer. Al-Sameea maintains that he is innocent, as his lawyer states the erroneous attributes of charges, due to child's small size and limited physical power.[34]

---

[31] "Chapter IV Human Rights." *UN.* 2014. https://treaties.un.org/pages/viewdetails.aspx?chapter=4&src=treaty&mtdsg_no=iv-4&lang=en

[32] "Bahrain Prosecution Office Orders for Detention of Children." *Shia Post,* 22nd March, 2014. http://en.shiapost.com/2014/03/22/bahrain-prosecution-office-orders-for-detention-of-children/

[33] "13 Bahrainis, Teens among Them, Get Life Sentence for Protest." RT, 31st March 2014. http://rt.com/news/bahraini-protesters-life-sentence-361/

[34] "11 Year-Old Children, Other Minors Detained in Bahrain." *Shia Post,* 28th May 2014. http://en.shiapost.com/2014/05/28/11-year-old-children-other-minors-detained-in-bahrain/

May 21st: In the village of Sitra, 14 year old Sayed Mahmoud Shubbar was murdered by Bahraini police forces. Shubbar was shot in the head, at close range, while grieving his condolences at the funeral of Ali Faisa al-Akrawil who had recently been killed by Bahraini police force. [35]

May 22nd: Bahraini teenager dies during clash with police. 15 year old Mahmoud Mohsen died as result of severe wounds sustained from birdshot pellets.

July 19th: A Bahraini court ordered the detention of 11 year old Jihad Al-Sameea for an unspecified period or until his "behavior improves" in charges relating to the ongoing political crisis in which citizens are consistently targeted for taking a stand for democracy.[36]

October 14th: Bahrain activist Zainab al-Khawaja arrested on accounts of "insulting the king" by allegedly publicly tearing up his photo. Zainab, who is currently 8 months pregnant, is set to face trial on 5 different charges. [37]

October 27th: Bahraini authorities detain 24 year old Zahra Al-Shaikh, along with her 6 month old son as she entered the al-Hodh al-Jaf prison to visit her husband who was recently jailed. Al-Shaikh's husband is being held on charges relating to alleged arson. Al-Shaikh and her infant are being held on terrorist related charges of participating in an illegal protest, also known as participating in an anti-regime peaceful assembly. Al-Shaikh's son, Hussein Habib Mubarak, 6 months old, is not receiving required medical treatment. Mubarak was born premature and has since dealt with numerous health difficulties causing a weakened immune system. Mubarak requires a special diet; however, the prison is unwilling to adhere to this, although they will not comment on why. Over the last 2 years, Al-Shaikh has consistently been detained for similar charges, inherently expressing the brutal regimes systemic repression.[38]

November 14th: Bahraini authorities summon and arrest 13 year old Bahraini citizen on charges relating to participating in illegal protests and igniting fire.[39]

November 30th: 14 year old, Mohammed Mansoor was arrested during a systemic raid of his home. During the raid, Bahraini police officers confiscated photos and phones, as well as broke down the door to the home. Mansoor was taken to the CID where he was subject to harsh torture, including that of being handcuffed and blindfolded while forced to stand for long periods, as well as was subject to electric shocks in order to distract a testimony. Mansoor denied all charges. This denial caused him to be taken back to the CID where he was subject to further torture in continuous attempt to distract a false testimony. Mansoor's mother confirms that once allowed to visit, there were visible signs of torture including that of bruises on Mansoor. [40]

---

[35] "Bahraini Regime Forces Kill Teenager in Sitra." *Shia Post, 21st May, 2014.* http://en.shiapost.com/2014/05/21/bahraini-regime-forces-kill-teenager-in/

[36] "11 Year-Old Children, Other Minors Detained in Bahrain." *Shia Post,* 28th May 2014. http://en.shiapost.com/2014/05/28/11-year-old-children-other-minors-detained-in-bahrain/

[37] "Pro-Democracy Activist Zainab Al-Khawaja Arrested in Bahrain." *Shia Post,* 15th October, 2014. http://en.shiapost.com/2014/10/15/pro-democracy-activist-zainab-al-khawaja-arrested-in-bahrain/

[38] "Mother and Infant Son Detained on Freedom of Assembly Charges in Bahrain." *ADHRB.* 20th, November, 2014. http://adhrb.org/2014/11/mother-and-infant-son-detained-on-freedom-of-assembly-charges-in-bahrain/

[39] "Support the Deposit Charged with Illegal Assembly in the Juvenile Detention Center." *Alwasat,* 14th November, 2014. http://www.alwasatnews.com/4451/news/read/935931/1.html

[40] "<<Bahraini Human Rights>>: Detainee was Tortured after He Was Arrested from His Home. " *Alwasat News.* 30th November, 2014. http://www.alwasatnews.com/4467/news/read/940625/1.html

The Right to Citizenship

In signing onto the International Declaration of Human Rights in 1998, Bahrain agreed to abide to the international notion that every human being has the right to citizenship as stated within the following articles:

Article 13.

(1) Everyone has the right to freedom of movement and residence within the borders of each state.

(2) Everyone has the right to leave any country, including his own, and to return to his country.

Article 15.

(1) Everyone has the right to a nationality.

(2) No one shall be arbitrarily deprived of his nationality nor denied the right to change his nationality.[41]

Furthermore, Bahrain ratified the International Covenant on Civil and Political Rights in 2006, making the following Bahraini law:

Article 12.

1. Everyone lawfully within the territory of a State shall, within that territory, have the right to liberty of movement and freedom to choose his residence.

2. Everyone shall be free to leave any country, including his own.

3. The above-mentioned rights shall not be subject to any restrictions except those which are provided by law, are necessary to protect national security, public order (ordre public), public health or morals or the rights and freedoms of others, and are consistent with the other rights recognized in the present Covenant.

4. No one shall be arbitrarily deprived of the right to enter his own country.[42]

However, since the uprisings of 2011 Bahrain has yet to implement these actions, further resulting in the revoking of numerous citizenships for Bahraini's who were unjustly accused and unfairly tried. The following are documented cases within 2014.

---

[41] "The Universal Declaration of Human Rights." United Nations, N.D. http://www.un.org/en/documents/udhr/

[42] "Chapter IV Human Rights." *UN.* 2014. https://treaties.un.org/pages/viewdetails.aspx?chapter=4&src=treaty&mtdsg_no=iv-4&lang=en

April 23ʳᵈ: Bahraini officials yet again systemically repress Shia Muslims exemplified in the deportation of Hussein al-Najati, a leading Shiite cleric. Al-Najati, a born citizen of Bahrain, is the Bahrain representative of Grand Ayatollah Ali al-Sistani, Iraq's most powerful Shiite figure. The Bahrain Ministry of Affairs contended that the deportation of al-Najati was justified in his lack of transparency and communication with Bahraini officials. Al-Najati was an influentially presence force at anti-regime rallies. The Ministry further revoked citizenship of al-Najati indefinitely.

August 24ᵗʰ: Protestors take to the streets as Al-Wefaq (Bahraini opposition party) express concerns over Bahrain's ongoing Naturalization Project.

November 21ˢᵗ: Three men were imprisoned, stripped of their citizenship and sentenced to 10 years of prison each, amid accusations of planning to attack the regime in August of 2013. [43]

The Right to Education

In 1992 Bahrain ratified the Convention on the Rights of the Child (CRC), thereby forcing the articles within the CRC into law. [44] Bahrain also signed on to the Universal Declaration of Human Rights (UDHR) in 1998, agreeing to abide to the following articles:

Article 26.

(1) Everyone has the right to education. Education shall be free, at least in the elementary and fundamental stages. Elementary education shall be compulsory. Technical and professional education shall be made generally available and higher education shall be equally accessible to all on the basis of merit.

(2) Education shall be directed to the full development of the human personality and to the strengthening of respect for human rights and fundamental freedoms. It shall promote understanding, tolerance and friendship among all nations, racial or religious groups, and shall further the activities of the United Nations for the maintenance of peace.

(3) Parents have a prior right to choose the kind of education that shall be given to their children.

Furthermore, Bahrain ratified the International Convention on Civil and Political Rights in 2006, intended on backing the UDHR and CRC. Thus, Bahrain has forced the enforced the following principles into law:

---

[43] "Bahrain Jails Three Activists, Strips Them of Nationality." *Gulf News.* 21ˢᵗ November, 2014. http://gulfnews.com/news/gulf/bahrain/bahrain-jails-three-activists-strips-them-of-nationality-1.1415880

[44] See Convention on the Rights of the Child.

Article 26.

(1) Everyone has the right to education. Education shall be free, at least in the elementary and fundamental stages. Elementary education shall be compulsory. Technical and professional education shall be made generally available and higher education shall be equally accessible to all on the basis of merit.

(2) Education shall be directed to the full development of the human personality and to the strengthening of respect for human rights and fundamental freedoms. It shall promote understanding, tolerance and friendship among all nations, racial or religious groups, and shall further the activities of the United Nations for the maintenance of peace.

(3) Parents have a prior right to choose the kind of education that shall be given to their children.

Although Bahrain has publically made a name for themselves by signing onto dozens of treaties and documents, including the creation of the Bahrain International Commission of Inquiry (BICI) in 2012,[45] intendant on documenting violations that took place after the uprising of 2011 in order to submit widespread reform, Bahrain has since to do so. Thus, leading to the following documented cases of persecuted children who lost access to their rights to education because of Bahrain's corrupt regime.

Cases of Children Who Lost the Right to Education:

May 30th: Bahraini authorities arrest 17 year old Sayed Jihad on charges of participating in an illegal gathering and committing rioting acts. Jihad claims that there were no protests taking place in Sar village at the time. He contends that he was peacefully sitting outside a shops door at the time of the arrest. Jihad had disappeared, unable to speak to his family for nearly 48 hours after arrest and will be unable to take his final exams. [46]

June 9th: Reports conclude that over 200 students under the age of 18 are currently incarcerated and denied their legal right to participating in education.

July 2nd: Bahraini authorities stall in legal obligations contending that they allow detained minors to partake in school exams. Of these students, Hussain Sahwan, (who is supposed to be graduating in the summer of 2014) has been unable to participate in the last 4 exams. Others, including Mohammed Issa Jassim (9th grade), have had their family send letters demanding that Jassim be granted his legal right to partake in exams but have not received a reply.

The Right to Employment

In expression of Bahrain's public notion of signing onto the Universal Declaration of Human Rights in 1998, they committed to adopt the following principles:

---

[45] See BICI.

[46] "Battle with Children Continues in Bahrain, Another Teen Arrested." Shia Post, 5th June 2014. http://en.shiapost.com/2014/06/05/battle-with-children-continues-in-bahrain-another-teen-arrested/

Article 23.

(1) Everyone has the right to work, to free choice of employment, to just and favourable conditions of work and to protection against unemployment.

(2) Everyone, without any discrimination, has the right to equal pay for equal work.

(3) Everyone who works has the right to just and favourable remuneration ensuring for himself and his family an existence worthy of human dignity, and supplemented, if necessary, by other means of social protection.

(4) Everyone has the right to form and to join trade unions for the protection of his interests.

Article 24.

Everyone has the right to rest and leisure, including reasonable limitation of working hours and periodic holidays with pay.

Article 22.

Everyone, as a member of society, has the right to social security and is entitled to realization, through national effort and international co-operation and in accordance with the organization and resources of each State, of the economic, social and cultural rights indispensable for his dignity and the free development of his personality.

Article 27.

(1) Everyone has the right freely to participate in the cultural life of the community, to enjoy the arts and to share in scientific advancement and its benefits.

(2) Everyone has the right to the protection of the moral and material interests resulting from any scientific, literary or artistic production of which he is the author.

However, since the uprisings of 2011, the Bahrain regime has enforced systemic repression on its citizen in a variety of ways. One of the ways the regime has decided to repress Bahraini citizens has been in the implementation of the Bahrain Naturalization Project in which the regime has moved to grant numerous foreigners citizenship, while denying their current citizens their basic right in prospects of ridding the country of the Shia Muslim majority.[47] The following are examples of documented cases of violations of the right to employment Bahrain has inflicted upon its citizens.

Cases of Bahraini Citizens Being Denied the Right to Employment:

August 28th: Indigenous Bahrainis excluded from private and public sector jobs. [48]

---

[47] See Bahrain Naturalization Project.

[48] "Indigeneous Bahrainis Excluded from Private and Public Sector Jobs." Shiite News, 28th August, 2014. http://www.shiitenews.com/index.php/bahrain/11314-indigenous-bahrainis-excluded-from-private-and-public-sector-jobs

The Right to a Fair Trial

Bahrain signed onto the Universal Declaration of Human Rights (UDHR) in 1998, complying that they would adhere with the following standards:

Article 6.

Everyone has the right to recognition everywhere as a person before the law.

Article 7.

All are equal before the law and are entitled without any discrimination to equal protection of the law. All are entitled to equal protection against any discrimination in violation of this Declaration and against any incitement to such discrimination.

Article 8.

Everyone has the right to an effective remedy by the competent national tribunals for acts violating the fundamental rights granted him by the constitution or by law.

Article 10.

Everyone is entitled in full equality to a fair and public hearing by an independent and impartial tribunal, in the determination of his rights and obligations and of any criminal charge against him.

Bahrain also ratified the International Covenant on Civil and Political Rights in 2006, making the following procedures to conduct trials Bahraini law:

Article 14.

1. All persons shall be equal before the courts and tribunals. In the determination of any criminal charge against him, or of his rights and obligations in a suit at law, everyone shall be entitled to a fair and public hearing by a competent, independent and impartial tribunal established by law. The press and the public may be excluded from all or part of a trial for reasons of morals, public order (ordre public) or national security in a democratic society, or when the interest of the private lives of the parties so requires, or to the extent strictly necessary in the opinion of the court in special circumstances where publicity would prejudice the interests of justice; but any judgement rendered in a criminal case or in a suit at law shall be made public except where the interest of juvenile persons otherwise requires or the proceedings concern matrimonial disputes or the guardianship of children.

2. Everyone charged with a criminal offence shall have the right to be presumed innocent until proved guilty according to law.

3. In the determination of any criminal charge against him, everyone shall be entitled to the following minimum guarantees, in full equality: (a) To be informed promptly and in detail in a language which he understands of the nature and cause of the charge against him;

(b) To have adequate time and facilities for the preparation of his defence and to communicate with counsel of his own choosing;

(c) To be tried without undue delay;

(d) To be tried in his presence, and to defend himself in person or through legal assistance of his own choosing; to be informed, if he does not have legal assistance, of this right; and to have legal assistance assigned to him, in any case where the interests of justice so require, and without payment by him in any such case if he does not have sufficient means to pay for it;

(e) To examine, or have examined, the witnesses against him and to obtain the attendance and examination of witnesses on his behalf under the same conditions as witnesses against him;

(f) To have the free assistance of an interpreter if he cannot understand or speak the language used in court;

(g) Not to be compelled to testify against himself or to confess guilt.

4. In the case of juvenile persons, the procedure shall be such as will take account of their age and the desirability of promoting their rehabilitation.

5. Everyone convicted of a crime shall have the right to his conviction and sentence being reviewed by a higher tribunal according to law.

6. When a person has by a final decision been convicted of a criminal offence and when subsequently his conviction has been reversed or he has been pardoned on the ground that a new or newly discovered fact shows conclusively that there has been a miscarriage of justice, the person who has suffered punishment as a result of such conviction shall be compensated according to law, unless it is proved that the non-disclosure of the unknown fact in time is wholly or partly attributable to him.

7. No one shall be liable to be tried or punished again for an offence for which he has already been finally convicted or acquitted in accordance with the law and penal procedure of each country.

Article 15.

1 . No one shall be held guilty of any criminal offence on account of any act or omission which did not constitute a criminal offence, under national or international law, at the time when it was committed. Nor shall a heavier penalty be imposed than the one that was applicable at the time when the criminal offence was committed. If, subsequent to the commission of the offence, provision is made by law for the imposition of the lighter penalty, the offender shall benefit thereby.

2. Nothing in this article shall prejudice the trial and punishment of any person for any act or omission which, at the time when it was committed, was criminal according to the general principles of law recognized by the community of nations.

Article 16.

Everyone shall have the right to recognition everywhere as a person before the law.[49]

However, although Bahrain has publically agreed to comply with the previous articles, they have expressed gross violations pertaining to conducting fair trials since the uprisings of 2011, fixated on repressing those who speak out against the corrupt regime. The following are documented cases of unfair trials that took place within 2014.

Cases of Unfair Trials in Bahrain:

June 3rd: Bahraini courts sentence 21 anti-regime protestors to 15 years imprisonment each amid the ongoing crackdown on the countries dissent.

July 1st: A Bahraini court sentenced 18 year old Akbar Ali al-Kishi to 65 years imprisonment for his participation in an anti-regime protest.[50]

August 14th: Bahrain courts sentences over a dozen Human Rights Activists to life in prison for their participation in protests against the Al-Khalifa regime.[51]

September 30th: Bahrain courts sentence 9 protestors to life imprisonment. [52]

November 20th: Bahraini courts sentence three Shia activists to imprisonment, totaling a stark 30 years. Each activist was sentenced to serve a ten year sentence on charges of what Bahrain authorities deem "terrorist" acts, concentrated on allegedly plotting an assault on Bahraini officers back in August.[53]

November 21st: On Friday, just before the November 22nd elections are set to take place (the first happening in nearly 3 years), as protestors flood the streets in protest of the corrupt regime, police forces infuse them with teargas. Amid numerous Bahraini citizens, is the general consensus that the elections are destine to fail, as they are filled with merely as much corruption as the everyday happenings in Bahrain themselves. [54]

December 1st: Bahrain courts sentence human rights defender, Maryam al-Khawaja to a one year prison sentence in her absence. Due to the fact that the regime seems to be incapable of producing fair trials, Maryam al-Khawaja neglected to be at her hearing today, but rather is seeking asylum from outside the country.[55]

---

[49] "Chapter IV Human Rights." *UN.* 2014. https://treaties.un.org/pages/viewdetails.aspx?chapter=4&src=treaty&mtdsg_no=iv-4&lang=en

[50] "Bahraini Teenage Protestor Sentenced to 65 Years in Jail." *Shia Post,* 1st July, 2014.

[51] "Bahrain Court Sentences Shia Activist to Life in Jail." *Shiite News,* 14th August, 2014. http://www.shiitenews.com/index.php/bahrain/11083-bahrain-court-sentences-shia-activists-to-life-in-jail

[52] "Bahrain Gives Life Sentences to 9 Protestors." *Shia Post,* 30th September, 2014. http://en.shiapost.com/2014/09/30/bahrain-court-gives-life-sentences-to-9-protesters/

[53] "Bahrain Court Sentences Shia Activists to Imprisonment." *Shiite News,* 21st November, 2014. http://www.shiitenews.org/index.php/saudi-arab/item/11971-bahrain-court-sentences-shia-activists-to-imprisonment

[54] "Bahrain Troops Attack Anti-Regime Pro-Democracy Protestors." *Shia Post.* 21st November, 2014. http://en.shiapost.com/2014/11/21/bahrain-troops-attack-anti-regime-pro-democracy-protesters/

[55] "Bahrain Sentences Activist to One-Year Prison Term." *Shiite News.* 2nd December, 2014. http://www.shiitenews.org/index.php/shiitenews/bahrain/bahrain-sentences-activist-to-one-year-prison-term

The Right to Freedom of Expression

By signing onto the Universal Declaration of Human Rights (UDHR) in 1998, Bahrain publically admitted to the recognition of the inherent right of all individuals regardless of creed, race, gender or age the right to publically express their opinions, as documented within the following articles:

Article 19.

Everyone has the right to freedom of opinion and expression; this right includes freedom to hold opinions without interference and to seek, receive and impart information and ideas through any media and regardless of frontiers.[56]

Bahrain also ratified the International Covenant on Civil and Political Rights (ICCP) in 2006, further recognizing these principles by signing them into Bahraini law as adhering to the following articles:

Article 19.

1. Everyone shall have the right to hold opinions without interference.

2. Everyone shall have the right to freedom of expression; this right shall include freedom to seek, receive and impart information and ideas of all kinds, regardless of frontiers, either orally, in writing or in print, in the form of art, or through any other media of his choice.

3. The exercise of the rights provided for in paragraph 2 of this article carries with it special duties and responsibilities. It may therefore be subject to certain restrictions, but these shall only be such as are provided by law and are necessary:

(a) For respect of the rights or reputations of others;

(b) For the protection of national security or of public order (ordre public), or of public health or morals.[57]

However, since the uprisings of 2011 in which Bahraini citizens have publically denounced the corrupt Al-Khalifa regime, the Bahrain kingdom has fiercely overlooked these principles in the systemic repression denying Bahraini citizens their inherent right to the freedom of expression. The following are documented cases that took place in Bahrain in 2014 in which individuals were either denied or persecuted on a basis of disregarding their right to freedom of expression.

Cases of Bahraini Citizens Being Denied the Right to Freedom of Expression:

---

[56] "The Universal Declaration of Human Rights." *United Nations,* N.D. http://www.un.org/en/documents/udhr/

[57] "Chapter IV Human Rights." *UN.* 2014. https://treaties.un.org/pages/viewdetails.aspx?chapter=4&src=treaty&mtdsg_no=iv-4&lang=en

June 7th: Yacoub Al-Slaise, political activist and leader of the Open Youth Coalition, was arrested on June 7th, 2014 on charges of insulting the regime via twitter; Trial has been postponed until October 13th.

September 3rd: Unconstitutional imprisonment of the chairman of Bahrain Teachers Association, Mahdi Abu Deeb on a basis of expressing opinion regarding that a recent disbursement of scholarship unfairly distributed funds, rejecting Shia majority students. [58]

September 9th: Ghada Jamsheer, Women's Rights Defender, scheduled to be tried in 10 separate cases on charges of insulting the regime via tweets and blog (which has subsequently been banned in Bahrain) by advocating to stand up for Bahraini women's rights.

October 23rd: Bahraini courts sentences blogger, Nader Abdulemam on charges of "insulting a religious figure" via a tweet posted to his Twitter account. Abdulemam was sentenced to serve a six month term in a Bahraini prison. [59]

October 23rd: Bahraini courts summon and arrest Sayed Jameel Khadem, who serves at the elite leader of the Bahrain's main opposition party, Al-Wefaq, Shura Council to appear before a Bahraini court on charges relating to a supposedly offensive tweet. Sources contend that the public prosecution summoned Khadem in order to interrogate him for allegedly interrupting the upcoming elections via a twitter post in which he contended that candidates are receiving "100,000 BHD to participate in the elections" (ADHRB). [60]

October 28th: Bahraini officials suspend rights of opposition political party just before election's (November 22nd).

The Right to Freedom of Religion

In 1998, Bahrain signed onto the International Declaration of Human Rights (UDHR) acknowledging that they recognize the following articles as inherent rights to all individuals:

Article 18.

Everyone has the right to freedom of thought, conscience and religion; this right includes freedom to change his religion or belief, and freedom, either alone or in community with others and in public or private, to manifest his religion or belief in teaching, practice, worship and observance. [61]

Following this recognition, Bahrain ratified the International Convention on Civil and Political Rights, adhering the following principles into Bahrain law:

---

[58] "Al Wefaq's Education Department Calls for Release of Abu Deeb." *Al Wefaq,* 3rd September, 2014. http://alwefaq.net/cms/2014/09/03/32147/

[59] "Imprisonment Rare Abdulemam 6 Months Because of the Tweets << << Twitter." *Alwasat,* 23rd October, 2014. http://www.alwasatnews.com/4429/news/read/930523/1.html

[60] "Tweets of Political Money >> Kazim beautiful lead for>> <<prosecutors>> Today." *Alwasat,* 23rd October, 2014. http://www.alwasatnews.com/4429/news/read/930536/1.html

[61] "The Universal Declaration of Human Rights." United Nations, N.D. http://www.un.org/en/documents/udhr/

Article 18.

1. Everyone shall have the right to freedom of thought, conscience and religion. This right shall include freedom to have or to adopt a religion or belief of his choice, and freedom, either individually or in community with others and in public or private, to manifest his religion or belief in worship, observance, practice and teaching.

2. No one shall be subject to coercion which would impair his freedom to have or to adopt a religion or belief of his choice.

3. Freedom to manifest one's religion or beliefs may be subject only to such limitations as are prescribed by law and are necessary to protect public safety, order, health, or morals or the fundamental rights and freedoms of others.

4. The States Parties to the present Covenant undertake to have respect for the liberty of parents and, when applicable, legal guardians to ensure the religious and moral education of their children in conformity with their own convictions.

Article 2.

In those States in which ethnic, religious or linguistic minorities exist, persons belonging to such minorities shall not be denied the right, in community with the other members of their group, to enjoy their own culture, to profess and practise their own religion, or to use their own language.[62]

However, since the uprisings of 2011, Bahrain has failed to not only implement but even recognize the inherent rights of all individuals, particularly that within the Shia Muslim majority. The following are cases that took place within Bahrain in 2014 in which Bahraini citizens were persecuted on a basis of Shia faith.

Cases of Bahraini Citizens Being Denied the Right to Freedom of Religion:

March 24th: Bahraini police forces fire tear gas at mourners of a funeral inside a mosque in the village of Sanabis. Sources confirm that no one was really sure why forces entered the mosque in the first place.

May 26th: Bahraini authorities manifest another regime cruelty towards Shia Muslims by permitting a Roman Catholic Church to be built in the same place that was occupied by a Shia Mosque only a year ago.

June 2nd: Bahraini authorities express systemic repression against Shia Muslims by turning famous Shia mosque into playground. Sources contend that the destruction of Abu-Thar Al-Ghufari Mosque has generated intense divide among Bahraini citizens. Sources further confirm that 30 mosques in all have been destroyed, all pertaining to the Shia sector of Islam. [63]

June 3rd: Bahraini authorities demolish 33 Shia mosques under pretext that they have been unlicensed since 2011, the time the uprisings began resulting in reprisal of systemic repression.[64]

62 "Chapter IV Human Rights." *UN.* 2014. https://treaties.un.org/pages/viewdetails.aspx?chapter=4&src=treaty&mtdsg_no=iv-4&lang=en

63 "Bahrain: The Authorities Continue to Oppress the Shia Sect." *Bahrain Rights,* 2nd June 2014. http://www.bahrainrights.org/en/node/6904

64 "Bahrain: The Authorities Continue to Oppress the Shia Sect." *ABNA,* 3rd June 2014. http://www.abna.ir/english/service/bahrain/archive/2014/06/03/613249/story.html

September 5ᵗʰ: Bahraini women banned from wearing traditional religious dress, abayas, to work. [65]

September 10ᵗʰ: Bahraini government has released plans to turn Shia Mosque into tourist attraction.

September 28ᵗʰ: Sheikh Mohammed Mansi prevented from travel to Mecca to perform Haji. [66]

October 19ᵗʰ: Prominent Bahraini political leader, Jasim al-Saeedi, a previous member of parliament, insulted Bahraini Shia Muslims inferring that any who gathered in 2011 in protest of peaceful democratic reform were criminals and Zoroastrian (an insulting term aimed towards Shia Muslims). Although many complaints have been made against al-Saeedi, dating back as far to 2005 before the 2011 revolution, no action has been made to hold al-Saeedi accountable. [67]

October 23ʳᵈ: Bahraini police force fire teargas canisters and live ammunition at peaceful teen protestors who gather with their religious flags in protest of the corrupt regime. Sources state that several protestors were injured. [68]

October 31ˢᵗ: Bahrain authorities repress Shia Muslims UDHR right of freedom of religion and freedom of expression as they forcefully dispersed teargas while tearing down the flags raised by Shia mourners in honor of the third Imam. [69]

The Right to Healthcare

By signing onto the Universal Declaration of Human Rights (UDHR) in 1998, Bahrain publically announced its decision to recognize the following articles as inherent rights of all individuals:

Article 25.

(1) Everyone has the right to a standard of living adequate for the health and well-being of himself and of his family, including food, clothing, housing and medical care and necessary social services, and the right to security in the event of unemployment, sickness, disability, widowhood, old age or other lack of livelihood in circumstances beyond his control.

(2) Motherhood and childhood are entitled to special care and assistance. All children, whether born in or out of wedlock, shall enjoy the same social protection.

Even though Bahrain publically announced this notion in adhering that they would make these basic rights available to all Bahrain citizens, the corrupt Al-Khalifa regime has failed to implement these manners since the uprisings of 2011.

---

[65] "Bahrain Minister's Anti-Abaya Decision Anulled." *Gulf News,* 5ᵗʰ September, 2014. http://gulfnews.com/news/gulf/bahrain/bahrain-minister-s-anti-abaya-decision-annulled-1.1381125

[66] "Sheikh Forgotten Prevent from Leaving for Haji following the Repercussion of the Decision to Prevent Him from Speaking." *Alwasat,* 28ᵗʰ September, 2014. http://www.alwasatnews.com/4404/news/read/924284/1.html

[67] "Saidi Calls on the Community in Bahrain, He Describes Palmjus and Criminals." *Alwasat,* 19ᵗʰ October, 2014. http://www.alwasatnews.com/4425/news/read/929439/1.html

[68] "Bahrain Revolution: The Suppression of the March Banners Hussein Weapon Shotgun and Toxic Gases Jacket and Religions." *Twitter,* 23ʳᵈ October, 2014. https://twitter.com/sitra_media/status/525627219155353600

[69] "MOI Orders Removing of Hussaini Flags and Banners." *Shia Post,* 31ˢᵗ October, 2014. http://en.shiapost.com/2014/10/31/moi-orders-removing-of-hussaini-flags-and-banners/

Thus, the following are documented cases of Bahraini citizens being denied their basic right to healthcare on a basis of the regime conducting religious systemic repression in prospects of maintaining power.

Cases of Bahraini Citizens Being Denied their Inherent Right to Healthcare:

September 24th: Detained prisoner denied medical access, mother subsequently pleas to the UN for care in which if continued rebuttal, the detainee could lose his sight. [70]

October 15th: Bahraini prison inmate is denied medical access to treat his severe health condition. The wife of a man arrested and sentenced to a ten year prison sentences states that her husband suffers from severe headaches as a result of a post-surgery side effect he underwent nearly 5 years before his imprisonment. She further contends that he consistently faints in the jail due to low blood pressure; however, authorities are unwilling to do anything but rather confiscate the man's medicine during cell searches.

October 22nd: 23 year old Hussein Jassim Isa is being denied basic human rights inside Bahraini prison. Isa, who was convicted on several accounts including allegedly attempting to escape from prison, has a combined prison sentence of 33 years. Isa's father contends that since his son's sentence, he has consistently been denied basic human rights, such as access to sunlight, being able to buy goods from the jail convenient store and denied basic medical treatment. He further states that Isa has also been subject to harsh amounts of unsanitary solitary confinement for the majority of his served sentence. [71]

The Right to Life

In 1998, Bahrain signed onto the Universal Declaration of Human Rights (UDHR) thereby abiding them to the following principles as stated within the UDHR:

Article 3.

Everyone has the right to life, liberty and security of person.[72]

Furthermore, Bahrain has also ratified the International Covenant on Civil and Political Rights (ICCPR) in 2006, thereby making the following articles subject to international law in Bahrain:

Article 6.

1. Every human being has the inherent right to life. This right shall be protected by law. No one shall be arbitrarily deprived of his life.

---

[70] "Bahraini Mother Pleads to UN to Provide Medical Care to Detained Son." *Shia Post,* 24th September, 2014. http://en.shiapost.com/2014/09/24/bahraini-mother-pleads-to-un-to-provide-medical-care-for-detained-son/

[71] "The Father of the Young Man was sentenced to 33 Years and Drop the Sexual Demands Unzip Solitary Confinement." *Alwasat.* 22nd October, 2014. http://www.alwasatnews.com/4428/news/read/930282/1.html

[72] "The Universal Declaration of Human Rights." *United Nations,* N.D. http://www.un.org/en/documents/udhr/

2. In countries which have not abolished the death penalty, sentence of death may be imposed only for the most serious crimes in accordance with the law in force at the time of the commission of the crime and not contrary to the provisions of the present Covenant and to the Convention on the Prevention and Punishment of the Crime of Genocide. This penalty can only be carried out pursuant to a final judgement rendered by a competent court.

3. When deprivation of life constitutes the crime of genocide, it is understood that nothing in this article shall authorize any State Party to the present Covenant to derogate in any way from any obligation assumed under the provisions of the Convention on the Prevention and Punishment of the Crime of Genocide.

4. Anyone sentenced to death shall have the right to seek pardon or commutation of the sentence. Amnesty, pardon or commutation of the sentence of death may be granted in all cases.

5. Sentence of death shall not be imposed for crimes committed by persons below eighteen years of age and shall not be carried out on pregnant women.

6. Nothing in this article shall be invoked to delay or to prevent the abolition of capital punishment by any State Party to the present Covenant.[73]

However, since the uprisings of 2011, Bahrain has failed to recognize both the UDHR and the ICCPR, among other documents. Thus, resulting in the persecution of thousands of Bahraini citizens, particularly of the Shia majority as documented in the following cases:

---

[73] "Chapter IV Human Rights." *UN*. 2014. https://treaties.un.org/pages/viewdetails.aspx?chapter=4&src=treaty&mtdsg_no=iv-4&lang=en

January 26ᵗʰ: 19 year old Fadhil Abbas Muslim dies due to severe wounds sustained from live ammunition. Muslim sustained wounds from security forces arbitrarily opening fire during protest two weeks earlier. Furthermore, sources confirm that Muslim's family was denied access to visit him in the hospital before his death.

February 12ᵗʰ: 52 year old Asma Hussain dies after falling victim to the systemic repression of the corrupt Bahraini regime. Hussain died shortly after falling unconscious in reprisal of severe beatings received from Bahrain militia. Hussain had attempted to stop Bahraini authorities from arresting her son, after heavily armed forces raided her home in search of him. In retaliation, Bahrain forces harshly beat Hussain causing her to fall unconscious resulting in later death. Furthermore, forces refused to tend to Hussain even after her sons consistent pleading.

February 19ᵗʰ: Bahraini courts sentence a Shia protestor to death and 6 others to life imprisonment on allegations of the killing of a Bahraini police officer back in 2013. Furthermore, 2 other protestors have been given 5 and 6 year sentences relating to similar charges. [74]

April 4ᵗʰ: 27 year old Abdul-Aziz al-Abbar dies from wounds sustained from clash with police during protest nearly two months ago. Al-Abbar's family says he was hit by a teargas canister and shotgun pellets. Of the pellets fired, one penetrated al-Abbar's brain while another hit his eye. Both pellets were shot at close range. Sources confirm that al-Abbar was in a coma at the hospital up to his death.

April 21ˢᵗ: Abdul Aziz Moussa Al-Abbar dies after being in a coma for 53 days sustained from injuries inflicted by the Bahraini authorities. Al-Abbar's family confirms that Al-Abbar's death was due to a critical brain injury sustained form being shot with a teargas canister directly in the head, as well as shotgun pellets. It is contended that these injuries were brought on during a protest in which the police used excessive force to suppress individuals protesting the corrupt regime. Furthermore, the death certificate released ensured that the cause of death was due to internal bleeding of the brain; however, failed to mention how Al-Abbar's injuries were sustained.[75]

May 21ˢᵗ: While attending the funeral of Ali Faisal al-Akrawi, who was recently murdered in a blast near his home on May 16ᵗʰ, Seyyed Mahmoud Seyyed Mohsen was killed by Bahraini police forces.

May 21ˢᵗ: Bahraini forces killed 15 people, including a teenage boy whose chest was torn by birdshot pellets, during a lethal raid in Sitra. The child died from heart and chest wounds sustained by a shotgun at close range.

May 21ˢᵗ: Police use excessive force of lethal weapons in order to suppress anti-regime protestors, resulting in the death of 15 year old Sayed Mahmood Sayed Mohsen. Mohsen was shot at close range with birdshot pellets tearing through his chest, resulting in lethally injuring both the boy's chest and heart.

May 21ˢᵗ: Youth killed in clash with Bahraini authorities during fight that broke out in the midst of a ceremony to mark the death of a Shia killed in recent explosion.

[74] "A Court in Bahrain Sentences a Protestor to Death and Six Others to Life in Prison." *Youtube,* 19th February, 2014. http://www.youtube.com/watch?v=hktk2pW8Vs0

[75] "Bahrain: Civilian Shot by Police with Teargas Canister Dies After Two Month Coma." *Bahrain Rights,* 21ˢᵗ April, 2014. http://www.bahrainrights.org/en/node/6836

December 9th: Bahraini citizen Abdul Karim al-Basri killed in explosion. Bahraini authorities have accused Bahraini opposition party, Al-Wefaq as being responsible for the bombing in aggregating the evidence to a "terrorist attack."[76]

December 29th: Bahraini citizens Mohammed Ramadan and Husain Ali Moosa are sentenced to death for their alleged involvement in a bombing that resulted in the death of a Bahraini police officer in February of 2014. Sources report that both men are being charged in adherence to false testimonies distracted under means of brutal torture. [77]

The Right to Peaceful Assembly

In signing onto the Universal Declaration of Human Rights (UDHR) in 1998, Bahrain publically expressed its recognition of the rights of all individuals within the following articles:

Article 20.

(1) Everyone has the right to freedom of peaceful assembly and association.

(2) No one may be compelled to belong to an association.[78]

By further ratifying the International Covenant on Civil and Political Rights (ICCP) in 2006, Bahrain enforced the following articles into international law:

Article 21.

The right of peaceful assembly shall be recognized. No restrictions may be placed on the exercise of this right other than those imposed in conformity with the law and which are necessary in a democratic society in the interests of national security or public safety, public order (ordre public), the protection of public health or morals or the protection of the rights and freedoms of others.[79]

However, with the uprisings of 2011 against the cruel Al-Khalifa regime, Bahraini security forces have continuously executed systemic repression by force in inflicting harm upon peaceful protests, resulting in many injuries and death as documented in the following cases that took place in 2014.

Cases of Bahraini Citizens Being Denied the Right of Peaceful Protest

February 4th: Police use excessive force on peaceful protestors, firing live ammunition, dispersing teargas and arresting several Bahraini citizens.

---

[76] "Bahraini Funeral Turns into Anti-Regime Protest." *Shia Post,* 12th December, 2014. http://en.shiapost.com/2014/12/12/bahraini-funeral-turns-into-anti-regime-protest/

[77] "NGO's Condemn Death Penalty Sentence of Mohammed Ramadan and Husain Ali Moosa. *Americans for Democracy and Human Rights in Bahrain,* 30th December 2014. http://adhrb.org/2014/12/ngos-condemn-death-penalty-sentence-of-mohammed-ramadan-and-husain-ali-moosa/

[78] "The Universal Declaration of Human Rights." *United Nations,* N.D. http://www.un.org/en/documents/udhr/

[79] "Chapter IV Human Rights." *UN.* 2014. https://treaties.un.org/pages/viewdetails.aspx?chapter=4&src=treaty&mtdsg_no=iv-4&lang=en

February 4th: Police use excessive force on peaceful protestors, firing live ammunition, dispersing teargas and arresting several Bahraini citizens.

February 26th: Bahraini authorities disperse teargas and rubber bullets in retaliation of peaceful protesting that took place in the village of Daih, west of the capital of Manama. Demonstrators were gathering in condemnation of the death of 23 year old Jaffer al-Durazi who had died at the hospital the previous day due to wounds sustained from Bahraini authorities. [80]

February 28th: Hundreds of demonstrators take to the streets in Bahrain, fighting with security forces in marking the third anniversary of the Arab spring inspired uprising of 2011. Sources confirm that there still appears to be no sign of resolve, as street protests are a daily occurrence and opposition leaders have failed to advance a political settlement that would grant Shiites more influence in the government. [81]

March 18th: Bahraini courts sentence Sayid Kamil A Hashimi to 3 years imprisonment. Hashimi is charged with insulting the king by means of advocating for the freedom of expression and religion among Bahraini citizens.

March 22nd: Bahraini forces disperse teargas onto thousands of protestors outside Manama who gathered in efforts of demonstrating against sectarian discrimination of Shia Muslims. [82]

May 18th: Chaos breaks out in clash between anti-regime protestors and police during funeral of al-Akwrawi. Police use excessive force to suppress protestors.

May 25th: Bahraini forces fire tear gas canisters and rubber bullets at peaceful protestors gathered in demonstration of individuals arrested for organizing and/or taking part in anti-regime protests, also cited as an act of terrorism under Bahraini law.

June 20th: Bahraini regime forces fire tear gas at protestors in the village of al-Daih, located west of the capital of Manama, as well as in several villages in the island of Sitra.

August 21st: Dozens of protestors arbitrarily shot down with bullets and infused with tear gas. [83]

August 27th: Protestors are shot with rubber bullets and infused with tear gas after protesting regimes ongoing Naturalization Project. [84]

August 27th: Bahrain regime forces brutalize protesters using rubber bullets and tear gas.

September 1st: Dozens of protestors permeated with teargas during a gathering to mark a year since a teenage protestor was lethally shot by Bahraini police forces while attending a religious ceremony.

---

[80] "Bahrain Accused Over Detainee's Death in Hospital." *BBC,* 26th February, 2014. http://www.bbc.com/news/world-middle-east-26358083

[81] "Bahrain Protests: Three Years On and Nothing Has Changed." *Huffington Post,* February 28th, 2014. http://www.huffingtonpost.co.uk/2014/02/28/bahrain-protests-three-year-aniversary_n_4873048.html

[82] "Bahrain Shias Protest against Government." *Aljazeera,* 22nd March, 2014. http://www.aljazeera.com/news/middleeast/2014/03/bahrain-shias-protest-against-government-201432234146582423.html

[83] "Bahrain Forces Use Tear Gas, Rubber Bullets against Protesters." *Shiite News.* 21st August, 2014. http://www.shiitenews.com/index.php/bahrain/11184-bahrain-forces-use-tear-gas-rubber-bullets-against-protesters

[84] "Bahrain Regime Forces Brutalize Protesters." *Shiite News.* 27th August, 2014. http://www.shiitenews.com/index.php/bahrain/11300-bahrain-regime-forces-brutalize-protesters

September 19th: Police use unnecessary means on protestors, inflicting teargas upon them. [85]

September 27th: In Eker, protests turned violent as police forces clash with protestor's arbitrarily unleashing rubber bullets and teargas. [86]

October 16th: Police violently attack protestors who took to the streets in Bahrain in avocation of the release of Nimr al-Nimr, a human rights activist recently sentenced to death in Bahraini ally, Saudi Arabia. [87]

November 12th: Bahrain authorities use forceful means to break up anti-regime protests.[88]

November 13th: Bahrain authorities disperse teargas on peaceful protestors demanding the release of 8 arbitrarily incarcerated women. [89]

November 16th: Bahrain forces arbitrarily inflict teargas on protestors in Eker, Bahrain who were peacefully demanding the release of the now 13 incarcerated women.[90]

November 19th: Police attack protesters in response to boycotting the upcoming November 22nd elections. Brutal forces inflicted teargas and rubber bullets upon the crowd to disperse them.[91]

November 19th: A Bahraini citizen loses his left eye as a result of being struck in the face with a teargas canister. The victim, Yousif al-Badah also sustained a fractured jaw and nose while participating in a protest that marked the anniversary of his son's death, who had been killed by Bahraini military.[92]

November 22nd: On Saturday, amid the many protests taking place throughout the streets of Bahrain in protest of the corrupt elections, security forces clashed with anti-regime protestors, infusing tear gas on them.[93]

November 25th: On Tuesday in Manama, just days after the November 22nd elections, Bahraini troops attacked protestors firing rubber bullets and infusing the streets with teargas. Witnesses are stating that police forces took photos of the ID cards of everyone present at the protests outside the house of prominent Shia cleric, Sheikh Issa Qassin, whose house was raided upon permission of inspection of suspected bomb. One can't help but wonder if the ID cards taken are advantageous to the continuous systemic repression of any Bahraini Shia's the police suspect may be involved in anti-regime protests. [94]

---

[85] Bahraini Police Forces Fire Tear Gas at Peaceful Protesters." *Shiite News.* 19th September, 2014. http://www.shiitenews.com/index.php/bahrain/11675-bahraini-police-fire-tear-gas-at-peaceful-protesters

[86] "Bahrainis Demand Release of Political Prisoners." *Shiite News.* 27th September, 2014. http://www.shiitenews.com/index.php/bahrain/11808-fg

[87] "Bahrain Police Attack Shia Cleric Nimr Supporters." *Shia Post.* 16th October, 2014. http://en.shiapost.com/2014/10/16/bahrain-police-attack-shia-cleric-nimr-supporters/

[88] "Anti-Regime Protests Continue in Bahrain." *Shiite News.* 13th November, 2014. http://www.shiitenews.org/index.php/saudi-arab/item/11770-anti-regime-protests-continue-in-bahrain

[89] "Regime Forces, Protestors Clash in Bahrain." *Shiite News.* 13th November, 2014. http://www.shiitenews.org/index.php/saudi-arab/item/11799-regime-forces-protesters-clash-in-bahrain

[90] "Bahrainis Protest Regime's Detention of Activists." *Shiite News. 17th November, 2014.* http://www.shiitenews.org/index.php/saudi-arab/item/11874-bahrainis-protest-regime-s-detention-of-activists

[91] "Bahrainis Voice Opposition to Forthcoming Elections. 20th November, 2014. http://www.shiitenews.org/index.php/saudi-arab/item/11952-bahrainis-voice-opposition-to-forthcoming-elections

[92] "Weekly Report- 17 to 23 November." *ADHRB.* 25th November, 2014. https://gallery.mailchimp.com/e6f34c0956184788aedb2040c/files/Weekly_Report_17_23_November.pdf

[93] "Bahrain Security Forces Clash with Anti-Regime Protestors." *Shiite News.* 23rd November, 2014. http://www.shiitenews.org/index.php/saudi-arab/item/12018-bahrain-security-forces-clash-with-anti-regime-protesters

[94] "Al Khalifa Regime Forces Attack Bahraini Protesters." *Shiite News.* 26th November, 2014. http://www.shiitenews.org/index.php/saudi-arab/item/12102-al-khalifa-regime-forces-attack-bahraini-protesters

November 26ᵗʰ: In Sitra, Bahraini security forces arbitrarily fire rubber bullets and infused crowds with teargas. Protestors were gathered in protest of the corrupt Al-Khalifa regime.[95]

December 1ˢᵗ: Protestors were attacked with rubber bullets and teargas as they took to the streets in commemoration of Yousef Baddah. Baddah lost his eye last month in a protest as a result of being hit by a teargas canister infused into the crowd. Yousef was participating in a protest in remembrance of his 11 year old son Ali, who was brutally murdered by regime forces in 2011. Ali died as a result of injuries sustained crushing his chest as a police vehicle ran him over and pushed him into a wall.[96]

December 12ᵗʰ: Bahraini police forces clashed with protestors during a demonstration that took place at the funeral procession of Bahraini citizen, Abdul Karim al-Basri. Al-Basri was killed December 9ᵗʰ in an explosion that Bahraini authorities amounted to a terrorist attack on the Bahrain regime. Sources confirm that Bahrain authorities dispersed teargas upon the protestors.[97]

December 19ᵗʰ: Protestor injured in clash with police forces. [98]

December 31ˢᵗ: Bahraini authorities infuse teargas on crowds that gather in protest of arbitrary arrest of Al-Wefaq leader Sheikh Ali Salman. Sources report that at least 5 people were injured in clash. [99]

The Right to Privacy

In 1998, Bahrain signed onto the International Declaration of Human Rights (UDHR), publically declaring that they recognize the following articles as International law:

Article 12.

No one shall be subjected to arbitrary interference with his privacy, family, home or correspondence, nor to attacks upon his honour and reputation. Everyone has the right to the protection of the law against such interference or attacks.

Article 14.

(1) Everyone has the right to seek and to enjoy in other countries asylum from persecution.

(2) This right may not be invoked in the case of prosecutions genuinely arising from non-political crimes or from acts contrary to the purposes and principles of the United Nations.[100]

---

[95] "Bahrain's Hold Anti-Regime Demo in Sitra." *Shia Post.* 27ᵗʰ November, 2014. http://en.shiapost.com/2014/11/27/bahrainis-hold-anti-regime-demo-in-sitra/

[96] "Regime Forces Attack Protestors in Bahrain." *Shiite News.* 3ʳᵈ December, 2014. http://www.shiitenews.org/index.php/shiitenews/bahrain/regime-forces-attack-protesters-in-bahrain

[97] "Bahraini Funeral Turns into Anti-Regime Protest." *Shia Post,* 12ᵗʰ December, 2014. http://en.shiapost.com/2014/12/12/bahraini-funeral-turns-into-anti-regime-protest/

[98] "Bomb Blast in Bahrain Village Injures Three Policemen." *Shia Post,* 20ᵗʰ December, 2014. http://en.shiapost.com/2014/12/20/bomb-blast-in-bahrain-village-injures-three-policemen/

[99] "Clashes Break Out Outside Bahrain Opposition Leaders Home." *Shiite News.* 31ˢᵗ December, 2014. http://www.shiitenews.org/index.php/shiitenews/bahrain/clashes-break-out-outside-bahrain-opposition-leader-s-home

[100] "The Universal Declaration of Human Rights." *United Nations,* N.D. http://www.un.org/en/documents/udhr/

Furthermore, Bahrain ratified the International Convention on Civil and Political Rights in 2006, adhering that they made the following articles Bahraini law:

Article 17.

1. No one shall be subjected to arbitrary or unlawful interference with his privacy, family, home or correspondence, nor to unlawful attacks on his honour and reputation.

2. Everyone has the right to the protection of the law against such interference or attacks.[101]

However, since the mass uprisings of 2011, Bahrain has yet to adhere to these policies and principles, and has subjected numerous Shia Muslims to arbitrary interference with their privacy contingent upon the Sunni ruling minority repressing the Shia majority. The following are documented cases of arbitrary interferences of privacy in 2014 that took place in Bahrain.

Cases of Bahrain Citizens Being Denied the Right to Privacy:

August 7th: Bahrain government hack Human Rights Lawyers and Activists website using U.K. Spyware, Zello. [102]

September 3rd: After a breach in security, in which Bahraini officials allegedly hacked into several pro-democracy protestors cellphones, staging a sting, 15 peaceful protestors were declared "disappeared."

September 15th: More than 10 illegal home raids took place, with at least 7 individuals being reportedly arrested, 2 of which were youth. [103]

October 16th: Three Bahraini citizens and human rights activists', who have long sought asylum in Britain, social media accounts have been confirmedly hacked by Bahraini authorities via Finfisher.

October 24th: Police forces illegally raid Bahraini citizen's homes causing extensive damage. [104]

---

[101] "Chapter IV Human Rights." *UN.* 2014. https://treaties.un.org/pages/viewdetails.aspx?chapter=4&src=treaty&mtdsg_no=iv-4&lang=en

[102] "Bahrain Government Hacked Lawyers and Activists with UK Spyware." *Bahrain Watch.* 7th August, 2014. https://bahrainwatch.org/blog/2014/08/07/uk-spyware-used-to-hack-bahrain-lawyers-activists/

[103] "Bahrain: Over 10 Home raids, 7 Arrested." *Shiite News.* 16th September, 2014. http://www.shiitenews.com/index.php/bahrain/11603-bahrain-over-10-home-raids-7-arrested

[104] N.A. *Twitter.* N.D. https://twitter.com/hassanabdalnabi/status/525831778875887616

November 10th-16th: Americans for Democracy and Human Rights in Bahrain (ADHRB) report that during the week of November 10th-16th, 2014 nearly 60 homes were arbitrarily raided; along with 45 protests taking place with several resulting in severe injury sustained by Bahraini authorities among protestors in Daih, Eker, Barbar, and Ma'ameer. [105]

November 12th: Bahrain authorities illegally raided homes of 13 women without warrant, performing illegal body searches on several of the women. Upon court summons the next morning, the women were detained; including that of pregnant woman and a woman who was taken along with her six month old child, being unable to change the child's diaper for nearly 12 hours. It was further reported that these women were subject to harsh treatment, torture, and death threats during their detainment. Of the arrested individuals, the human rights activist further contends that several men were arrested on the same charges.[106]

November 25th: In the early morning hours of November 25th, just after the November 22nd elections, Bahraini authorities raided the home of top Shiite cleric, Sheikh Issa Qassin. On their twitter feed, Bahraini Interior Ministry stated that the raid was permitted by the leader of main opposition party, Al-Wefaq, in response to allegations of the cleric holding a bomb in his home. In response, hundreds of Bahraini citizens stood outside the house of Qassin in protest of this arbitrary raid. [107]

December 28th: Masked Bahraini authorities arrested 25 Shia Bahraini citizens during a mass raiding of 32 homes. [108]

Torture

In signing onto the Universal Declaration of Human Rights (UDHR) in 1998, Bahrain publically agreed to hold themselves to the standards set forth within the UDHR as follows:

[105] "Bahrain Weekly Newsletter #78." *ADHRB.* 18th November, 2014. https://gallery.mailchimp.com/e6f34c0956184788aedb2040c/files/Weekly_Report_10_16_November.pdf

[106] "Bahrain: Women Targeted in Mass Arrests over Popular Referendum." *ADHRB.* 14th November, 2014. http://adhrb.org/2014/11/bahrain-women-targeted-in-mass-arrests-over-popular-referendum/

[107] "Bahrain Police Raid House of Top Shiite Cleric." *Shiite News.* 25th November, 2014. http://gulfnews.com/news/gulf/bahrain/bahraini-police-raid-house-of-top-shiite-cleric-1.1417918

[108] "Masked Security Forces Arrest 25 Bahrainis in Sanabis, Aleker." *Shia Post,* 28th December, 2014. http://en.shiapost.com/2014/12/28/masked-security-forces-arrest-22-bahrainis-in-sanabis-aleker/

Article 5.

No one shall be subjected to torture or to cruel, inhuman or degrading treatment or punishment.[109]

Furthermore, after ratifying the International Covenant on Civil and Political Rights (ICCP) in 2006, Bahrain complied that they would admit the following articles into international Bahraini law:

Article 7.

No one shall be subjected to torture or to cruel, inhuman or degrading treatment or punishment. In particular, no one shall be subjected without his free consent to medical or scientific experimentation.[110]

However, since the uprisings of 2011, there have been numerous cases of documented torture that has taken place within the Bahraini prisons, leading to prolonged illness and even death. Furthermore, members of the royal family themselves have even been intendant on participating in the torture directly. The Al-Khalifa deny this accusation, however are unwilling to go to court to participate in a fair trial that would disprove the notion.

The following are documented cases from 2014 of torture that took place within Bahrain.

Cases of Torture in Bahrain Prisons:

February 26th: 23 year old Jaffar Mohammed Jaffar dies due to lack of treatment after extensive torture inflicted by Bahraini authorities. Jaffar's family confirms that he was subject to harsh beatings and electric shocks. Jaffar has sickle cell anemia and was denied treatment of disease. Sources further confirm the recent rise in death of citizens with sickle cell anemia, as an expert contends to the BBC that the intense use of tear gas on protestors could potentially play a role. The expert further states that the teargas could trigger severe problems for a sickle cell sufferers because it restricts the supply of oxygen and causes acute, temporary physical stress, often times leading to death if left untreated.

August 24th: Abdulhadi al-Khawaja, (currently serving life sentence in prison for plots to overthrow the regime) starts hunger strike in protest of ill treatment towards prisoners. [111]

August 27th: Surprise inspections of Juvenile Detention Centers unmask that prisoners are being severely ill treated, requiring immediate reform.[112]

---

[109] "The Universal Declaration of Human Rights." *United Nations,* N.D. http://www.un.org/en/documents/udhr/

[110] "Chapter IV Human Rights." *UN.* 2014. https://treaties.un.org/pages/viewdetails.aspx?chapter=4&src=treaty&mtdsg_no=iv-4&lang=en

[111] **"Sunday 24 August 2014, Bahrain - Joint Statement: Bahrain: Prominent Human Rights Defender Abdulhadi Al-Khawaja to Start a New Hunger Strike"** *Bahrain Rights.* 24th **August, 2014.** http://bahrainrights.org/en/node/7013

[112] "Detained Juveniles Require Special Measures." *Gulf News.* http://gulfnews.com/news/gulf/bahrain/detained-juveniles-require-special-measures-1.1377137

August 31st: Photojournalist, Ammar Abdul Rasool subject to severe torture and mistreatment over photograph he shot.[113]

September 4th: Bahrain authorities express systemic repression in the detainment of 17 year old photographer, Hussam Madhi Suroor. Sources verify that Suroor and his friend were disappeared and subject to torture for five days before being transferred to Dry Docks Juvenile Detention Centre. Before transfer, both Suroor and friend were taken to "unofficial torture center" known as Khayala, where they endured harsh beatings and ill treatment. Suroor has previously been detained in 2012 where photographs document severe wounds he received during detainment. Suroor was released days later without charges.

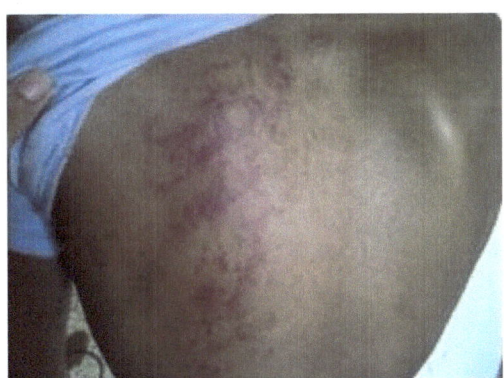 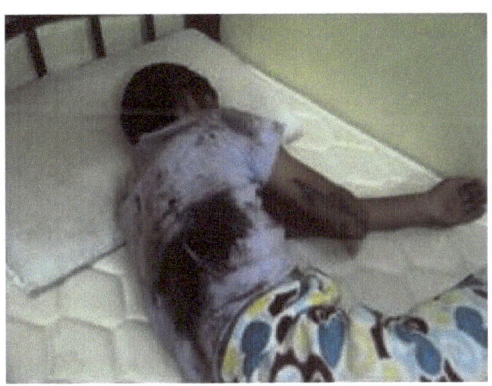

November 6th: Bahraini authorities torture Hasan Majeed al-Shaikh to a heinous death. Witnesses confirm hearing shrilling screams coming from the cell where al-Shaikh was beaten and later drug out after being pronounced dead. Al-Shaikh's family were allowed to view his body, confirming bruises, ruptured kidneys, and a broken jaw and skull. Family members were not allowed to take photographs. Sources confirm authority personnel involved in arbitrary beatings leading to death had posed early death threats to al-Shaikh, who was imprisoned for 10 years upon drug related charges, that he would not make it out alive.[114]

Other General UDHR of Bahraini Citizens Not Being Recognized

Article 2.

Everyone is entitled to all the rights and freedoms set forth in this Declaration, without distinction of any kind, such as race, color, sex, language, religion, political or other opinion, national or social origin, property, birth or other status. Furthermore, no distinction shall be made on the basis of the political, jurisdictional or international status of the country or territory to which a person belongs, whether it be independent, trust, non-self-governing or under any other limitation of sovereignty.

---

113 "Bahrain Photographer Ammar Abdul Rasool Subjected to Torture Over Photograph He Shot." *Bahrain Rights*. 31st August, 2014. http://bahrainrights.org/en/node/7027

114 "Inmate Reportedly Beaten to Death at Bahrain's Central Prison." *ADHRB*. 13th November, 2014. http://adhrb.org/2014/11/inmate-reportedly-beaten-to-death-at-bahrains-central-prison/

Article 4.

No one shall be held in slavery or servitude; slavery and the slave trade shall be prohibited in all their forms.

Article 16.

(1) Men and women of full age, without any limitation due to race, nationality or religion, have the right to marry and to found a family. They are entitled to equal rights as to marriage, during marriage and at its dissolution.

(2) Marriage shall be entered into only with the free and full consent of the intending spouses.

(3) The family is the natural and fundamental group unit of society and is entitled to protection by society and the State.

Article 17.

(1) Everyone has the right to own property alone as well as in association with others.

(2) No one shall be arbitrarily deprived of his property.

Article 21.

(1) Everyone has the right to take part in the government of his country, directly or through freely chosen representatives.

(2) Everyone has the right of equal access to public service in his country.

(3) The will of the people shall be the basis of the authority of government; this will shall be expressed in periodic and genuine elections which shall be by universal and equal suffrage and shall be held by secret vote or by equivalent free voting procedures.

Article 28.

Everyone is entitled to a social and international order in which the rights and freedoms set forth in this Declaration can be fully realized.

Article 29.

(1) Everyone has duties to the community in which alone the free and full development of his personality is possible.

(2) In the exercise of his rights and freedoms, everyone shall be subject only to such limitations as are determined by law solely for the purpose of securing due recognition and respect for the rights and freedoms of others and of meeting the just requirements of morality, public order and the general welfare in a democratic society.

(3) These rights and freedoms may in no case be exercised contrary to the purposes and principles of the United Nations.

Article 30.

Nothing in this Declaration may be interpreted as implying for any State, group or person any right to engage in any activity or to perform any act aimed at the destruction of any of the rights and freedoms set forth herein.

Conclusion

Since February of 2011, Bahraini citizens, particularly that of the Shia majority, have been subject to ill treatment by Bahraini forces on a basis of religious persecution inflicted in the form of systemic repression. Although many promises of reform have been initiated by the Bahraini government, persistent brutal treatment of Bahraini citizens has been carried out by not only the Bahraini military but also by its allies, Saudi Arabia and the United Arab Emirates. It is due to this continuous systemic repression that Bahraini citizens continue to protest for their rights as not only a Bahraini citizen, but as human beings, which the Kingdom of Bahrain deliberately fail to recognize and adhere to.

Amongst that, the Bahraini government persistently spends the most amount of money, globally, pursuant in covering up the crimes against humanity committed by their government in efforts of protecting their own egotistical interests. Furthermore, due to Bahrain being host to the U.S. Navy's Fifth fleet, as well as it's adherence to continuously advance the economic growth for nations such as the United Kingdom, international compliance and recognition have been little to none, in comparison with other Gulf states such as Syria or Lebanon.

It is for this reason, that human rights organizations, individuals and governments alike must come together to demand that the violence end. It is time to hold the Bahraini government accountable for their brutal actions in inflicting harm upon the Shia majority. As seen in the condemnation of Hitler in Germany, the massacres of Rwanda, and the current denunciation of Assad's inflicted genocide on the people of Syria, it is time to give Bahrain deserved prioritization in international politics, in the efforts and cooperation needed on behalf of the United Nations in demanding the immediate reform of the Bahrain government.

Recommendations

To the Government of Bahrain

- Employ the immediate and unconditional release of all prisoners of conscience,
- Conduct thorough investigations of treatment of prisoners in all Bahraini institutions, including the alleged "secret" ones. Furthermore, employ suggested reform and conduct fair trials of all persons involved in alleged accusations, including Royal family, military and members of parliament,
- End religious segregation by the rebuilding all destroyed mosques, returning jobs to persecuted citizens, restore all revoked citizenships and allow for continued education of all individuals who were forced to halt their education due to systemic repression;

To the United States and United Kingdom

Demand the immediate and unconditional release of all prisoners of conscience by:

- Barring all trades with Bahrain until reform is reached,
- Imposing travel bans on Bahraini Royal Family,
- Halting all U.S. initiated economic activity within the region, including freezing assets,
- Ending protection of Bahrain by U.S. and U.K. military;

To the United Nations Member States

- Employ immediate restrictions on all of Bahrain's rights until reform is issued,
- Arrange and issue release of all prisoners of conscience,
- Halt all military protection until reform is issued;

www.ingramcontent.com/pod-product-compliance
Lightning Source LLC
Chambersburg PA
CBHW060836290526
45792CB00006BB/1952